Some Humble Joy

Robert Hollins

Copyright © 2024 Robert Hollins
All rights reserved. ISBN: 979-8-89324-516-5
Printed in the United States of America.

No part of this publication shall be reproduced, transmitted, or sold in whole or in part in any form without the prior written consent of the author, except as provided by the United States of America copyright law. Any unauthorized usage of the text without express written permission of the publisher is a violation of the author's copyright and is illegal and punishable by law. All trademarks and registered trademarks appearing in this guide are the property of their respective owners.

The opinions expressed by the Author are not necessarily those held by the Publishers.

The information contained within this book is strictly for informational purposes. The material may include information, products, or services by third parties. As such, the Author and Publisher do not assume responsibility or liability for any third-party material or opinions. The publisher is not responsible for websites (or their content) that are not owned by the publisher. Readers are advised to do their own due diligence when it comes to making decisions.

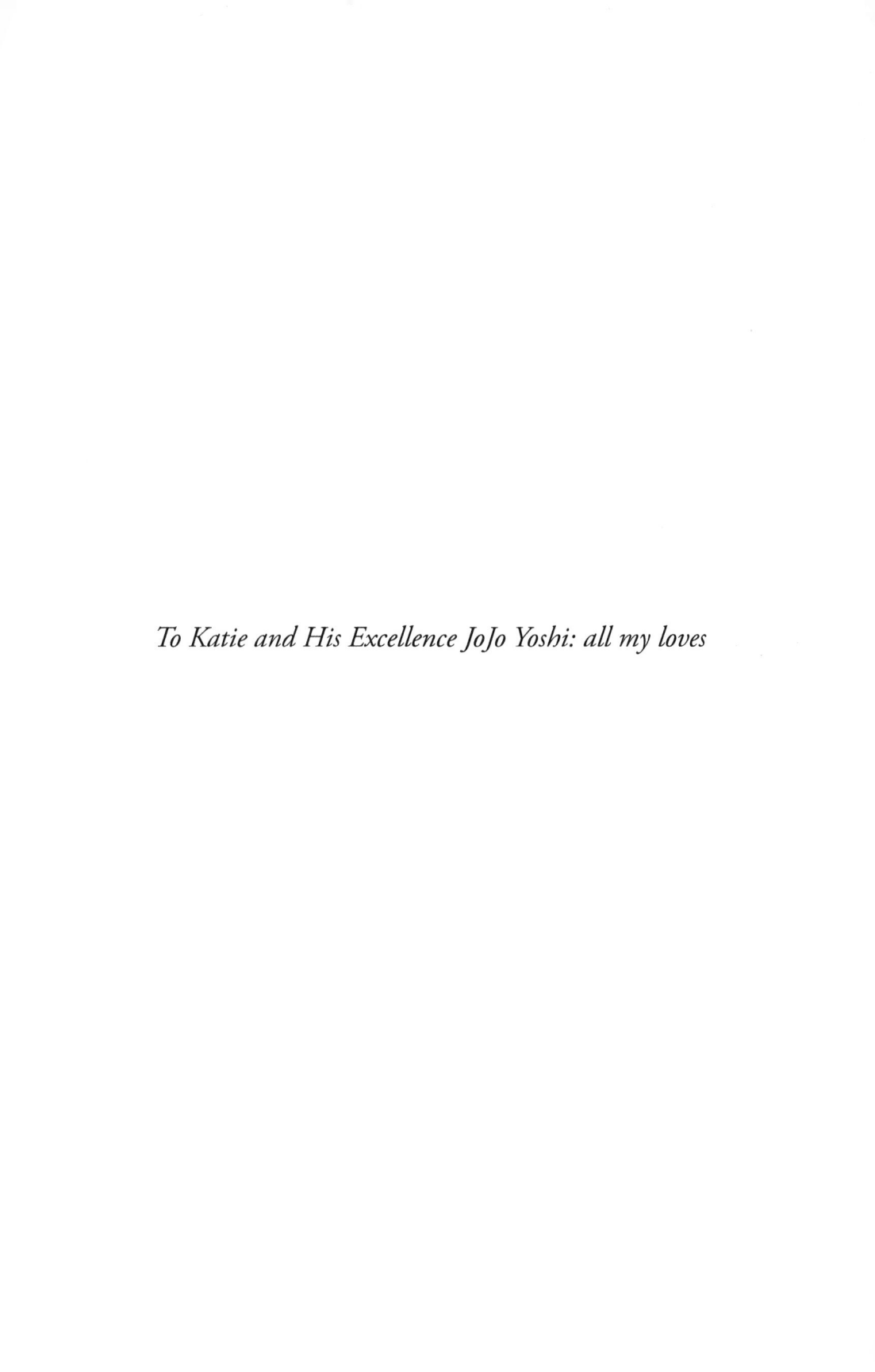

To Katie and His Excellence JoJo Yoshi: all my loves

Table of Contents

Bento intro	5
Let's call her Sheila	6
Too many lies/never the right time	8
Trouble in a baby tee	10
Melody	12
Titular experience	14
Heard she got big and moved into a slum	17
Dating age	19
Foreverstare	22
Watching the fan waiting for some sign	24
Vermillion	26
Americana	28
This ode to Ayalone	30

[Bento intro]

this isn't a call to arms or an errant fly ball

but rather

a chance let run free those missed opportunities

"rememberies"

a grasping chance

holding on as ever permits

some dreams need to dwindle, cuz

true passions burn

poking reveals a condensed jitterbugs size

leftover tingle of sprite-

how the colorful incandescence rushes forth

its gladness in the nights hold

stones of the path

warmth in the breeze

[Let's call her Sheila]

how dare you speak to me as if some person of interest

politely living your worth

interrupting the teachers' discourse

I should have disobeyed, looked longly into your eyes

past those lashes

listen to your lips breathing

let thoughts remember fingers

tease and pull your hair

feel your tiny perfect woman impress me

yeah, weird, but check it

I can only imagine

outstretching an open hand

pulling you into my safety as the bullet flew

you couldn't have drawn me out

~ Some Humble Joy ~

no fault

my dismissals such a clowning achievement

no harm

to have won and supported and loved and lead with you

learned to share, rather

the timing wasn't there

but that's why your memory liner

[Too many lies/never the right time]

some figures stand out not for their superiority

we imply a set of features deserving of high regard

a fulfilling completeness

paths cross because they have to want to need to interlace

must admit a near miss

recreation is faulted and never enjoyed

walked away encouraged, though

disgraced/thankful/shadowed

work a lifetime

try to impress, attempt to please

break everything

break to satiate such a woman such a catch

mademoiselle

Some Humble Joy

a lady capable of gracefully holding a bloody pulp of soul

her look of sleepy disdain at some minor disturbance

chills me calls forward riches to exploit

sex wasn't, was marginal, and was hers to be enjoyed

she held the prize

we just couldn't figure that out in time as

gone too soon, and

completely

[Trouble in a baby tee]

there's a reason Spike Lee wore those quarter-round glasses
this won't tell you why
look thru his library of work
allow yourself time to wake
realize how beautiful but normal them sistas be
nonchalantly preparing their arts
craft a seemingly mirrored reality
of course, look at the designer
but let's again allow our mentions to rest easy
and glide along with women of a nature fiercely
how does one describe the gait of any cat
each step belying claws and death and natural cruelty
hear woman
every shade of night, holding every quality of love

captured infinite depth

bear witness to the rainbow caught within the epidermis

tempt the subtle heat

follow the curves of delicate strength

be blessed with courtesy

honored by strict dismissal

charged by an elementally explosive neutron

and I say, make way

every time she enters your space

be quick as His heralds have made landfall

[Melody]

Robyn Aaliyah Mary Mariah Ill Na-Na Don Doja
fellow Christian ladies
so many tunes ...
the physical frequency of a vibe
think wave machine
as the sounds fly light speeds through my heart
and in that instant radiates warmth
calls to me
set tingling, a resonance, some kindred
the plucking of a string, dust off some half-worn boot
ladies, divas, stylists, voices on a breeze
didn't matter what I was wearing
the groove dressed me: styled in whispers
flexed the tongue

still so many more so many more of these feelings

sheer numbers swiftly defeat any notion of sensibility

look back at our social evolution, admitted or not

our flowering tower is constant

each layer each brick is a house

saying it goes round and round

incorporating the needs of the most

but all that's for another discussion

passing notion during the intermission

as I feel her eyes or some other intentions

on me

[Titular experience]

gotta get this back to basics

no more side-shanking stud nails, nope

slow and patient prevents cross-threading

transparency mode enabled.. my head is rather clear

hearing the sounds of wife telling stories to my son through the walls of our home

inertial memory returns to other hallways

I dunno who she was

there were fewer whom I could have cared less about

we were the safe place they needed

must have actively erased memories of her soon thereafter

for a lad, irreverence persists

a bred altruistic

for what actually is

Some Humble Joy

common sense

please, a pause

imagine a garbled cable chanel lol

volume on nill hoping for a split second of coherent skin

funny how the audio was ever crystal. And I gotta say

for a radio kid

the listening was hot and alien

I intruded

she was the alabaster trophy of budding womanhood

try to nonchalonatly fuss about, as the timid do

capture in effigy and make trophy prize

admiringly dust, from time to time

left to age on some topshelf

12 cubed-bit compression of memory filled

standing like a sequoia

"Close the door"

it wasn't a question

had to look my way to the ground

see the butler excuse himself from some unseen

kinda wish I could remember her eyes

actively rewriting history for a smile

[Heard she got big and moved into a slum]

it's not like I cared for anyone before

lust is love is interest is finite and fixed

I had never seen a woman sunbathe in a backyard before

all girls at some age qualify for womanhood

most don't bother with the applications

she could have been someone's chick, a goddess

mis americanitas, buenos

consider a Latina Crawford

better lips and longer

real, present

a checkered past is a finished race

the results of her living seemed contained in her eyes

in the dark brown lipstick and firmé attire

it never storms in the desert, like really

weather is consistent ¿como no?

there are subtleties across regions

so we were all alerted to the rolling thunder the voluminous purple-blue velvet clouds

her bedroom window picture-framed those layers

her bed was by the window

we watched the trailing edge of the advancing front

I guess she was already watching

the sky mirrored ebony tones off her face

I remember saying something

like the kind of something that's said out of innocence

recognizable as truth and historic yet amateur

look back at the storm before she see's you looking

I'll never forget those clouds

[Dating age]

different for everybody

time-place-motivations-desire-nerve all play a hand

but the clothes, the ride, the spare cash, the space

hungry enough to scoop out some plump plum pudding

hang for a few stories

see us in college

she was the hexed outsider everybody obviously ignored

and we hit it off

I bought her pancakes at an all night shop her eyes fluttered

we exchanged charged imaginations of fantasy and

ritual thriving

she shared her music

her bed was small

heart burned like fevers her body compelling

she? dumped me when i hit on her twin
many years go by, times change
I'm more together bills paid got nice wheels
looking to establish things
she was amazeballs. In fact
her whole circle of friends made me salivate
should have let more girls play with my hands back then
say something sweet with a smile
be open to translation and conversation
she was hit and lied to and was loosing her footing
my jam happened to be ready at an opportune moment
we both were between the last
I liked the tobacco staining her left cheek teeth
that little neck pocket holding her second and third chin
the pornstar worthy kisses she ladled on me

so many reasons

so when mental health was in jeopardy

she had to choose stability or me

don't dwell too long on the paths not taken, dearhearted

to move on is living

thriving

giving every chance to the whims of heyday hand-holding

framing spheres about the self

giving praise as the reinforcement of positivity in action

as deed clarifies the meaning of togetherness

whether for the night or just long enough

everybody misses the bus

insert your own analogy

It's the getting to where-ever you were going from

and back to where you've been for once

[Foreverstare]

there's a nothingness in the alone times
questions of "if it matters" humdinger
looking back doesn't help
it never eases the sentiment of closing doors
I think mom toted me about because I was always home
Learned much later she was the opposite
I don't know how or why i peaked too soon
or how I forgot such neat tricks
a subconscious clairvoyant
the work is clear. Yet, as part of the process
waiting for subtext's maturation through the medium-
will twist a nipple
an original theme urged acknowledgement
rehash the most relatable burning crosses

~ Some Humble Joy ~

remember when the alone was forgotten
remember when just me wasn't enough
remember to thank even the smallest interaction
keepsake collection level cherry pit diamond notions
loops having no context, no life of their own
this weight sits in my jaw and squares it
yokes me
creates its own damn backlog
within is the marvelous continuum
inspiring sloppy lips to shimmer and rush forth
refreshed
a gentle walk through a forest of once-barren lands
scattered the seeds during a forced match
somehow, I want to thank everyone
we know there's much more in store
many more lives to experience

[Watching the fan waiting for some sign]

why do we fret and worry

rehash the past

as if time travel through the mind's eye allows a redo

in that moment: exactly who we were and will be

just usually with less than what we would have wanted

there will be fewer still, regrets, I think, till again

time offers a replay

reminds of chosen directions toward summer sun

still hidden in the craft of some mooned night

hidden memories or rather hides realities eventually seen

to what end

life lived as worker cobbling a path using the brokens

admittedly, happy, at looks back

seeing the progress

this new way of paved

each of us some reflection of the eternal

some reason to rush as if onward

so similarly expressed different

nose-picking and nauseous

no settle no give

hands clenched into the aether

drifting

with a smile

[Vermillion]

floating in on a breeze

she drifted by and, with a cocky hand gesturing

something ladies in black and white films might offer

while smoking/ preparing for an evening

two moons and she's back, with reason

laughs at my ease

sitting close while a movie plays

I never learned to ask the smart questions

don't want to casually muck the water

and just barely panic when realizing how much danger I'm in

her being compelled by my willingness

I needed to find her

to run my hands over every square and find that hairline fissure

her fault, time and again

time and again
fairytales are based on real people and their mundane
as if carried within a dream
as toes brush the water's surface
living horrible lives of lies filled kinder surprises
we fought for something
each of us
wanted a thing that could be real
and met reality individually
she a mother, wife, lover
call me a spouse father figure
knotted, in some distant past
reflexively printing promises speaks to your timeline
handsful of silmaril tears
a true honor to have held such attention

[Americana]

the entire premise for our needing
to satisfy her monster
examples of prodigious consumerism
searching out some un-needed quantity
fleeting is the expression of luxury through goods
the establishment sets your place and price as gaurantee
aspiration is a token tradable for a tangible thing
leverage existence??
she demands an accountant's ledger of respects paid due
thrust into a spotlight of self-perception
her shared will controls who is chambered
as the clique sounds around, shines the one to fall into place
the moment is ambivalent
acutely rare and aware of stylized popularity

Some Humble Joy

for shame

we have demanded of said broken to be whored

in this case, applaud her righteous purity in deed

for this home was never broken

stolen, yes

squatted, yes

inversely adopted by way of guttered boulevards

I offer my arm and hold her hand aloft as we walk

festivities somewhere in trees. daylight

ghosted fire and laughter where it seems darkest

our perishable history, a bit of smoke

ever coy

I'd like to know where she's leading

learn her path is like water for the builders

this isn't the expected ending

[This ode to Ayalone]

impossible to know the real name

this gist of our shared concubine

she's been there

racing at me

laughing on heavy winds swirling the dust

rustling about the lost leftovers

carried and strewn in the wake of our living

a horrible grifter

looks back with death's black riddle glistening from rusted lips

adorable and integral to this being her floral chaos,,unexpected

and we get comfortable

stir-crazy and hot on the road: her calm hand rests atop mine

I realized. I assume.

Some Humble Joy

to those not so closely acquainted, she's a handmaiden
a contractor, an advisor
I met her too young
watched her mature as a neighbor, a sister
never a lover
to my chagrin, a best man, a best-kept secret
a lusty milf categorized in the worlds wide library
I want after her
feel a hunger in the spreading wake
never bashful or nude in such presence
this thick stream of consciousness jagged
and oblong with a recessed stair step downward
turning my back to her is rude
revealed is the dark sun of propulsion
revered is the persistence
we don't know if there can be an exchange

Milton Keynes UK
Ingram Content Group UK Ltd.
UKHW020132021224
451757UK00019B/174